Stronger Bodies, Sharper Minds

Importance of Sports in Everyday Life

Published by

Renu Kaul Verma

Vitasta Publishing Pvt Ltd

4348/4C, Ansari Road, Daryaganj

New Delhi - 110 002

 an imprint of Vitasta Publishing

ISBN: 978-81-19670-57-4

© Vitasta Publishing

First Edition 2025

MRP ₹395

Editor: Saumya Chaudhary
Book Design by Rohit Gautam
Printed by Vikas Computer and Printers

CONTENTS

Sports Play a Vital Role in Children's Development

Some Key Reasons

- **Physical Development:** Regular exercise through sports helps children build strong bones and muscles, develop coordination and motor skills, and maintain a healthy weight. It also establishes healthy habits that can last a lifetime.

- **Mental Health Benefits:** Physical activity releases endorphins and helps reduce stress, anxiety, and symptoms of depression. Team sports can boost self-esteem and provide a healthy outlet for emotional expression.

- **Social Skills Development:** Through sports, children learn essential social skills like

teamwork, leadership, and communication. They practice conflict resolution, learn to follow rules, and develop empathy by understanding and supporting teammates.

- **Academic Performance:** Studies show that regular physical activity improves concentration, memory, and cognitive function. Student-athletes often perform better academically due to improved focus and time management skills.

- **Character Building:** Sports teach valuable life lessons about perseverance, goal-setting, and handling both victory and defeat gracefully. Children learn that success comes through dedication and hard work.

- **Time Management:** Balancing sports with schoolwork helps children develop organisational skills and learn to prioritise tasks effectively.

- **Healthy Competition:** Through sports, children learn to compete in a structured, positive environment. This helps them develop resilience and cope with challenges in other areas of life.

- **Social Connections:** Sports provide opportunities to make friends outside of school and develop relationships with positive adult role models like coaches and mentors.

- **Cultural Understanding:** Team sports often bring together children from different backgrounds, helping them develop cultural awareness and respect for diversity.

- **Physical Health Awareness:** Sports help children understand their bodies better and develop awareness about nutrition, hydration, and the importance of rest and recovery.

ARCHIT AND NEHA'S VISIT TO THE SPORTS ACADEMY

CHAPTER ONE

It was the peak of summer holidays, and there was a general air of laziness in Neha and Archit's house. The brother and sister had spent most of the holidays inside the safe confines of their home, away from the blistering heat that made their head hurt. Since they had nothing to do, the siblings had grown restless and started fussing about the house. This irritated their mother, Shanti.

'Calm down!' Shanti yelled at her kids, 'I will have a headache by the end of the day because of the havoc you two have been creating since morning!'

'We are bored, Mom! You won't let us go outside because of the heat, so we have nothing to do all day!' Neha whined.

'I allowed you to go outside and play in the evening, but you both just chose to loiter around the stairs with your friends and do nothing! You have gotten very lazy, kids!'

Neha tried to argue but she realised that her mother was correct. She couldn't remember the last time she'd gone out and played with her friends. Even Archit, who used to be very active, and full of energy, looking for one hint to go outside and play, had become suddenly lethargic and unwilling to do anything.

'That's true, Mom! I don't understand what happened to us,' said Neha

Archit agreed with his sister and said, 'I still like to go out and play, but most of my friends just stay in their homes and are glued to their TVs or computers. What can I do, Mom?'

Shanti realised that Archit wasn't entirely wrong. She'd noticed that very few children played in the society's park now. She couldn't even blame the summer heat either, as this decline had been happening for several years. Suddenly, a sense of unease gripped her—what if her own children became addicted to modern gadgets and lost touch with the world around them?

She remembered her own childhood, and how she'd been an inter-school track athlete. She had excelled at sports all through her childhood, while also doing good in her studies. In her time, Shanti and her siblings had spent a lot of time playing outside, without any intrusion from their parents.

Indeed, her mother encouraged her to take part in track competitions at her school, which led her to win and take part in other games as well.

Shanti could not let her children become inactive. She wanted them to prosper in at least one sport so that they'd not only become physically fit but also learn to have discipline and resilience in life.

She spent the next few days researching the best sports academy to enroll them in. After a lot of research, she discovered the Lenin Sports Academy that had just opened near their locality. She went to its website and read about all the sports that the academy taught. Satisfied by the diverse array of sports, she called her kids to her room and asked them what sport they'd like to learn.

'Let me think,' Neha said with a hint of excitement, 'I need to see the list of sports they are offering before I can make up my mind.' Archit's interest also peaked as well.

Shanti gave her the list. Neha scanned the names of all the sports, but she still couldn't decide. Archit took the list from her and read it as well.

'I can't make up my mind! Please, Mummy, take us both to the academy and let us see all the children playing sports mentioned in the list! That will make it easier for us to decide what we want to learn!'

Shanti nodded, 'Okay, I will take both of you to the academy tomorrow. You can decide which sport you want to play after exploring all the options that are available at the academy.'

The next day, they all went to the Lenin Sports Academy. Neha and Archit were impressed by the place. It was part of a sports stadium, with a large playground behind the building. The academy had a gym for bodybuilding, a hall for yoga, and a swimming pool as well.

It was early evening, and children were milling around the complex, getting into lines for warm-up sessions.

Shanti asked her children, 'Can you spot and tell me the names of all the Sports activities that you can see, hmm?'

Archit and Neha looked around the playground and saw children practising different kinds of activities. From martial arts like taekwondo and karate to athletic events such as running, high jump, and long jump, as well as sports like football, cricket, volleyball, badminton, and tennis, the siblings observed a variety of activities. They watched both children and adults practising diligently on the grounds.

They told her the names of all the sports they could identify.

'Well done, and have you decided what you'd like to play?'

'I like running and cricket, but I don't know if I will be great at either,' said Archit.

Shanti understood what he meant. She remembered being young and getting very scared at the thought of playing a sport because she was uncertain if she would be good at it. Even after her parents assured her that sports was about more than just winning and losing, Shanti knew that nobody remembered the losers. It was a scary thought for a child to have, but she knew how to make Archit feel better.

Shanti said, 'It is very natural to feel scared while you are trying out a new thing, but remember, to become good at anything, you have to be disciplined. You have to put all of your efforts to master whatever sport you choose, and it doesn't matter if you win or lose. What matters is that you give it your all.'

Archit nodded.

He had said that he liked cricket because it was the most commonly played sport in India. Everyone was supposed to like cricket because India had the best cricket team in the world and it was a relatively easy sport that anyone could play even if they didn't want to be a professional cricketer. Archit had played cricket with his friends a lot of times and enjoyed it.

If he had to be honest with himself, the possibility of getting good at cricket was high, but actually making it professionally was alarmingly low. And despite his mother's insistence that winning and losing didn't matter, he knew that he had to be the best at what he did or else nobody would care that he played a popular sport in his free time.

'Hmm, I don't want to play cricket. Everyone I

know plays it already and I don't want to follow other people. I want to do something else. Mummy, can I go and get a closer look at what other kids are doing before I make a final decision?'

'Of course, you can go and talk to the coaches and see what sport suits you the best. Neha, you should go with him as well,' said Shanti.

The siblings left their mother and walked side by side to survey all the sports that were being played across the playground.

Their first stop was the badminton court. Neha grabbed a bit of the chain link fence that surrounded the court and leaned in to look at the two girls who were having a match. Drenched in sweat, with their mouths stretched out like rubber bands, the girls were going at each other with a gusto that surprised her. They were very fast, leaping into the air as if they had springs attached to the soles of their feet, their arms stretched out to hit the shuttlecock with their rackets. A sharp noise, like a 'thh-u-n-k', could be heard every time the cock smashed its corked head on the tight net of the rackets.

Neha was mesmerised by their athleticism. As she looked at them, transfixed by their play, Neha wondered how long the two girls had trained to get so good at the game. Clearly, a lot longer than an average girl who only played it for fun.

Suddenly, the girl on her right hit a smash, but the shuttlecock deviated in the air, spun wildly and fell before Neha's feet. She picked it up gingerly and threw it back. The girl caught the cock in a swift, sharp movement, but before she could turn back to the game, she looked at Neha curiously.

'Are you planning to join badminton classes?' she asked.

Neha opened her mouth to say something, but sputtered over her words. What was she supposed to say? She had come to see their game because it looked fascinating and she was impressed by their skills. That was it—she still hadn't decided which sport she wanted to choose.

'Uhh, I am just looking around,' said Neha. 'Trying to get an idea about all the sports that are taught here so I can choose the one I like the most.'

The girl smiled, and then turned to get back to her game.

Archit, who'd been watching the scene in silence, had similar appreciation for the two girls, but he knew that he didn't want to play badminton at all. He didn't feel suited for the sport, and wanted to play something more dynamic. He looked over his shoulder, and saw that at the opposite side of the ground, a few children were practising martial arts.

'Neha, I'm going to go and see what those kids on those blue mats are doing,' said Archit.

'You can look around on your own and see what you like.'

Neha watched her brother leave, then walked away from the badminton court and towards the tennis courts.

A panoply of high-pitched voices greeted Archit as he neared the area where the children were practising martial arts. Spread out on rows of blue and orange mats, the boys and girls were flinging their arms and legs in practised motions, and yelling a word again and again.

'Kiai!' they screamed furiously, turning on their heels and kicking high in the air.

Again, Archit was impressed by the dedication and the energy of the kids. He had watched a few Jackie Chan movies with his father and he had always been in awe of the acrobatics and martial skills that the actor possessed. While he watched Jackie kick a man in the face and then do a cartwheel with ease, Archit had wanted to learn his skills so that he could also use them if he ever faced bad people.

As the group of children continued to kick high and then punch in mid air, Archit's awe turned into a sense of fear. He saw how much focus and energy went into becoming a martial artist. These kids were not only enthusiastic about their sports, they had also spent hours practising the same motions until they perfected it. It seemed too hard, and suddenly Archit was overwhelmed by a fear that he'd never be able to become as good as these children if he started taking the classes. How embarrassing would it be for him and his parents if he was unable to do a full leg split or kick properly?

Sensei Khan, who was walking between the rows of children, saw a little boy looking at them, his eyes wide with wonder. He walked over to the boy and bent down to talk to him.

'So, you'd like to learn to be a fighter, eh?'

Archit blinked in surprise. He hadn't expected the master to notice him, let alone speak to him. Unsure of what to say, he stood there, frozen. The sight of the practice intrigued him, but a lingering fear gnawed at his mind—what if he wasn't good enough to become a skilled martial artist?

'Sir, how long does it take to become a good martial artist?' Archit asked him.

Sensei Khan took a long look at the boy and then responded, 'Well, that depends on how dedicated and disciplined you are. The journey of a martial artist never ends. It is ongoing, and continues till the end of his or her life. You learn new things as you go, and leave the old techniques in the past. Nobody becomes a master in a matter of days. Being a fighter, being able to kick and punch gives you a big responsibility to always practice caution and never use your power over people who are weaker than you. Karate isn't just a sport, it's a way of life. Anyone can learn how to fight, but only few can truly take the teachings of karate and transform themselves into true disciples.

Archit nodded solemnly. He was starting to get what Sensei Khan had said He also understood that he had made a mistake by only focusing on one part of martial arts.

Of course, it wasn't only about fighting! How could it be? Karate was meant to teach a person how to achieve inner and outer harmony. That surely couldn't be possible if one was always quarrelling with others and hurting them. But with years of learning, one could indeed become a master like Sensei Khan.

'Sir, how did you learn Karate?'

Sensei Rashid Ali Khan smiled as images of his past flashed across his eyes. His journey to become a Karate master had been very long and hard. It couldn't be summarised in one or two sentences as it had started when he was even younger than Archit.

'Come, sit on the mat, and I will tell you how learning karate changed my life and saved me.'

***

A FUN SPORTS FACT FOR YOU

Did you know that playing sports is like giving your brain a super-boost? When you run, jump, or throw a ball, your brain releases special chemicals that make you feel happy and help you think better in school!

SENSEI
RASHID'S
JOURNEY
CHAPTER
TWO

Rashid Ali Khan was born in the bustling region of Chandni Chowk in Delhi. A boisterous boy, he had always been very active and loved to go out and play with his friends. His parents always encouraged him to take part in sports because they felt that he could really succeed as a sportsman. Rashid's best friend, Kamal, was a studious boy who excelled in studies. They both went to the same school, and were at the top of their respective fields.

As it usually happens, a lot of children in their school were jealous of their achievements because they weren't as dedicated to their studies or towards extracurricular activities. They vented out their frustration by bullying Rashid and Kamal, and trying to get them into trouble. One of the worst bullies in their class was a boy named Manish. Brawny, but dim-witted, he and his friends, Soum and Preet used to name-call and beat Kamal and Rashid in the guise of having fun.

One day, the group cornered Kamal and Rashid at the end of school, and hit them on their faces by claiming that they had invented a new 'slapping game' and were testing on other children as well. Manish slapped Kamal so hard that his lip started bleeding. Seeing this, Soum and Preet ran away, while Manish kicked Rashid in the chest because he'd wanted to fight back against the unjust beating.

As they stumbled out of the school gates, Kamal started crying.

'I hate them!' he said viciously, 'I don't know why they always bully us. We have never done anything to them. I am always friendly with everyone in the class. I have never shown any kind of disrespect to anybody. But they think they can just say anything to me, hit me and then go about their day without getting any punishment from the teachers!'

This was true. The teachers in their school were entirely useless when it came to addressing bullying. They did not care at all if one of their students was being bullied. Rashid and Kamal knew this because they had actually gone to their principal with a letter and told him about their experiences. The principal had come to their class, looked around dismissively and told them to change their seats.

This didn't have any sort of effect on the bullies. What's more, it only increased the intensity, as Mohit had shoved Rashid's head into a wall when he realised that they had mentioned him prominently in the letter.

'They do it because they think we are weak and can't fight against them,' Rashid said. 'They are taking advantage of the fact that we don't want to hurt anyone. If we fought back, they would never be able to hurt us like this.'

'But how?' Kamal asked. 'I have seen you trying to fight Manish. He is taller and heavier than you. And then his two bodyguards are always around him. They hold you back if you try to fight back. We can't win against them!'

Both boys looked sad and felt very helpless. There was nobody around them who could teach them how to defend themselves. They were completely alone. If they told their parents about the bullying, they would surely do something about it, but there was no guarantee that it would ever stop.

No, they had to do it themselves.

But how?

Kamal's question kept echoing in Rashid's mind as he went home that day. Chandni Chowk was a very congested and lively place. It was known for its grand shops and eating places. Rashid knew that he'd have to look past the place where he lived if he wanted to find someone to teach him self-defense.

A new gym had opened at a place near his house. Rashid knew that children weren't allowed to go to gyms, but he hoped that he could find someone who'd help him find a good self-defense teacher somewhere in Delhi.

'Hmm, I don't know...' the owner of the gym, Raj said when Rashid asked him. 'I haven't heard of any self-defense classes that take place nearby, but I know a guy, Ajit, who has a brown belt in karate, who comes here during weekends. I will talk to him and let you know where he learnt karate from.'

Rashid didn't know much about karate, but he had seen action movies on the television with his father. He knew that karate was a form of self-defense martial art. He hoped that it was good enough to teach him how to defend himself and his friend against people like Mohit.

Wanting to speak to Ajit himself, Rashid waited till the weekend and then went to the gym to meet him.

His first impression of Ajit wasn't positive. With an average height, and thin form, Ajit didn't seem like anybody's idea of a skilful martial artist. But, as Rashid sat outside the gym and followed Ajit's movements through the glass doors, he was surprised by how powerful he was. He watched as Ajit kicked the body bag so hard that he sent it flying. He saw him dent the leather by punching it so furiously that his hands were just a brown blur.

Rashid was entranced by Ajit's quick and sharp movements. He was shocked how much power Ajit had in his slim body. There and then, he decided to learn karate and excel at it.

He approached Ajit as he was packing his gloves and introduced himself.

'You want to learn karate because you want to beat up your bullies?' Ajit asked.

'No, no. My friend and I want to learn it so that we can defend ourselves against them. We don't want to fight them, but if they keep attacking us, then we want to be prepared to fend them off.'

Ajit rubbed his chin and said, 'Hmm, okay, sure. I will give you the address of my dojo. Bring your parents with you so they can talk to my Sensei and arrange classes for you and your friend.'

Rashid sighed with relief. He knew that his parents would agree to his wish of learning karate, and they did. Similarly, Kamal's parents also enthusiastically permitted him to learn martial arts.

For the next few months, Rashid and Kamal poured every ounce of their energy into learning the basics of Karate. They spent a lot of time stretching, increasing their stamina and practising how to kick.

It wasn't very easy at first. There were times when they were so exhausted by the practice sessions that they wanted to just quit and run home. They also didn't get the techniques of kicking, and spent a lot of time just flinging their legs and hurting their toes.

Thankfully, they had a very good teacher, Sensei

Veer, who patiently taught them how to balance themselves while sending out a kick and punching without hurting their wrists.

Slowly but steadily, they mastered the basics and became skilled enough to kick high. Six months had passed since Rashid and Kamal began their karate journey, and they were already experiencing the benefits of learning martial arts. Their balance and power improved by leaps and bounds. After almost a year, Rashid and Kamal could kick high, with perfect stance and do a middle split on the floor without breaking a sweat.

Sensei Veer was very pleased by the two boys' progress. Rashid and Kamal felt it too. Their bullies, who'd laughed at them when they'd seen them practising on the school grounds, began to sense a tangible change in the two boys.

Then one day, Rashid and Kamal finally got the opportunity to show off their newly developed skills to their bullies.

It was the games period and everyone from their class was out and playing on the grounds. Rashid and Kamal, who'd not been picked to play football by their classmates, had decided to practise their kicks under the shade of the giant peepal tree that stood at the edge of their school boundary wall.

Everything was going well, until suddenly, the football came rolling to their corner.

'Hey, loser! Give back the ball!' Mohit yelled at them. Rashid looked down at the ball, then at Mohit's sweaty, leering face. There was a time when he would have complied and given back the ball without any protest. Mohit would've insulted him again for not kicking the ball properly and then hit him on the head as punishment for his incompetence. But that time was long past and Rashid was not going to obey his bullies anymore.

He walked to the ball, put his right foot on it and looked straight at Mohit.

'Get it yourself, Dumbo,' he yelled back, 'We are not your servants!'

For a moment, Mohit was genuinely shocked. He'd never expected anyone to question his authority, much less a weakling like Rashid.

'What did you say?' he roared, 'You want me to come and get the ball, you freak? Do you know what'll happen when I come there and take it from you?'

Rashid smirked. How had he ever been scared of this pathetic guy?

'Just come and take the ball, Mohit,' said Rashid, 'or are you too scared?'

Mohit's gang and the other boys from their class had stopped what they were doing and now stood listening to this showdown. They couldn't believe what they were seeing; that a meek boy like Rashid was challenging Mohit, who was brawny and a foot taller than him in height.

Kamal, who stood a little away from Rashid, silent so far also felt a surge of confidence in his chest. He looked at Rashid's determined face, ready to face their biggest opponent, and decided that he didn't want to remain scared anymore either. He'd face his fears head-on.

'What happened, you are still standing there? Do you want the support of your gang to just take a football back from us?' he said, snickering at Mohit's expression of disbelief.

This was a cry of war, and Mohit charged at them with a ferocity of a bull that had just spotted a red flag in the crowd.

Rashid had been waiting for this moment for months. He knew what to do because he'd practised it in his mind a number of times. As Mohit raced towards him, his face a deep angry red and his eyes bulging out of their sockets, Rashid took his stance and stood straight, keeping his opponent in clear line of sight. He knew that Mohit was heavier than him, but he'd seen even the lightest fighters win against bulky opponents because of their speed and agility. Mohit ran up to Rashid and flung his left arm in a quick arc to punch him. Unfazed by this, Rashid sidestepped, pivoted on his left foot, and raised a kick that caught Mohit in the face.

There was a loud slapping noise as the mud-caked sole of his shoe connected with Mohit's right cheek. Mohit didn't get a chance to stop and inspect what had happened to him. He spun in his spot, his vision a blurred whirlpool, and felt himself keel over, and fell splat on the ground.

Rashid put his right foot on the football and looked up at his classmates.

'Ouch,' he said.

Mohit let out a yelp, and stood up gingerly.

'What was that for?' he asked Rashid. 'There was no need to kick me so hard!'

'There was no need to run towards me as if you were going to punch me,' Rashid said, adding, 'I was just defending myself.'

Mohit grunted. He slapped his thighs to get the dust off his pants and turned to walk away.

'That's it?' Gaurav, his best friend, shouted, 'You aren't going to teach him a lesson, Mohit?'

'What lesson?' Mohit said, rubbing his cheek. It was going to bruise, and he was already trying to spin a story in his mind that'd satisfy his parents. 'You should fight him if you want! He'll kick you in the head so hard, your brain will fall out of your large mouth. Or whatever is stuffed up there that makes you such an idiot!'

Rashid kicked the ball lightly and it rolled off towards his classmates.

Naman, a boy who had never bullied him, picked it up and nodded at him.

'Okay, boys. Let's get back to the game!' he yelled, and threw the ball back into the ground.

Kamal and Rashid watched as an embarrassed Mohit got back to playing football. They didn't know what they felt. Rashid had finally defeated their bully and humiliated him so that Mohit would think twice before attacking them again. But somehow, this didn't feel like a victory. Even though Rashid had finally proven that he was more powerful than Mohit, he didn't really feel like he'd achieved something great.

'That's because karate is not about fighting your enemies,' Sensei Veer told them when he got to know about the incident.

At first, he'd wanted to scold Rashid for violating one of the sacred rules of karate. One must never pick a fight with someone who is clearly beneath their level of skill. One must never pick a fight just to show off his or her skill. One must never pick a fight with the intent to hurt someone.

Rashid had broken all the rules. He had hurt a fellow classmate and shown no remorse for his actions. This would have led to a clear and firm expulsion from the academy—if Sensei Veer hadn't first learned why Rashid had attacked Mohit.

Kamal had known that the fight would put Rashid in trouble. Even though Mohit hadn't told the teachers about it, because he didn't want to appear weak before anybody, Kamal was certain that Sensei Veer wouldn't approve of Rashid's actions.

So, he'd decided to tell the truth himself, along with the reason for Rashid's assault on Mohit.

Sensei Veer had listened to the story in silence, his expression neutral, neither dismissive of Mohit and Kamal's struggles, nor in support of their deeds.

'So that's why you both wanted to learn karate? To fight your bullies and prove that you could beat them,' he asked Kamal.

'No, Sensei. We wanted to learn karate to defend ourselves. We knew that nobody was going to help us, not even our teachers. They listened to our complaints and looked away. We couldn't talk to our parents because that wouldn't solve anything. We were being bullied even outside the school by other boys as well. We wanted to do something that'd put a stop to all this torture.'

Sensei Veer was quiet. He had not expected this. Usually, the boys who learnt karate at his dojo were always ready to show off their skills to people and intimidate their friends. It was a very childish thing to do, but understandable. Even he had done it in his childhood. But what Kamal told him was something very different. He wanted to comfort the boys for what they had suffered, but he couldn't let them go without a warning either.

He waited till the class was over, and then told Rashid and Kamal to meet him in his office.

'Yes, karate isn't about attacking someone who is less strong than you,' he told them. 'But, it is about defending yourself from people who are stronger than you. And those who trouble you as well. I can't say that what you did was right, but I can't fault you for protecting yourself against bullies either.

Similarly, although I can't punish you, I can't let you off either.'

At the end, Rashid and Kamal were given fifty laps to run before training for a week. This was a very harmless punishment for the fight, and they were glad that Sensei Veer had understood their situation.

After the incident, their classmates stopped bullying them and Rashid made sure that none of the other students had to go through the same treatment. He had absorbed the teachings of Sensei Veer, and never fought anyone outside of the dojo.

'That's how karate not only saved my life, but became my chosen profession,' Sensei Rashid said as he finished his tale.

Archit had listened to the story intently, and found that karate was the ideal sport for him. He wanted to become someone who protected the weak. Martial arts was a noble sport and it was good for physical as well as mental health.

He took a deep breath and told Sensei Rashid about his wish to learn karate.

***

NEHA'S CONFUSION

CHAPTER THREE

While Archit was being taught the principles of karate, Neha was wandering, looking for a sport to truly inspire and move her heart. So far, she had surveyed badminton, volleyball, football, basketball and tennis. All of them had tugged a little at her chest, but none had drawn her in. She was getting frustrated by the joyful exertions of the children around her who had happily chosen the sport they wanted to play and were excelling at it. Would she be able to do the same? Neha was desperate. What if there was no sport for her? What if she was meant to be boring and stay tied to academics?

Her steps hastening, Neha took a full circle of the ground and came to the back where some girls were playing hockey. She stopped at the edge of the field and decided to observe the game. Hockey was, after all, the national sport of India. And even though it didn't get much publicity, there was a lot of scope for it, as Neha had read in the news.

The girls swayed their hockey sticks over the cropped grass, their faces drenched in sweat. They were going through practice drills for the game.

Neha looked at the sweaty shins, and frizzy strands of hair that escaped from their ponytails. She was mesmerised by their coordination. She stepped closer and closer, until she had crossed the boundary of the field, and mistakenly knocked a bunch of hockey sticks that were standing bundled up.

'Oh, sorry!' Neha said, and knelt down immediately to fix her mistake.

The girls stopped their training and looked at the little child who was fussing over the hockey sticks. One of them, the eldest and the tallest, Priyanka, approached Neha.

'You seem new here,' she said.

Neha looked up at the tall girl, and let the hockey stick she was holding fall to the ground.

'Yes, Didi, I came with my mummy and brother to see what kind of sports I like.'

'And have you chosen the sport you like?' Priyanka asked her playfully.

'No, not yet,' Neha said. 'I can't tell which sport is best suited for me!'

Priyanka smiled.

'That's okay. You can just watch us and then go back to your mom.'

'Wait,' Neha said, 'How long have you been playing hockey, Didi?'

'Oh, I have been playing it since I was eight years old.'

'I'm eight years old as well!' Neha said. 'How did you start playing hockey, Didi?'

Priyanka looked back at her teammates. She had to go back to practice, but seeing the little girl had touched something in her heart. It didn't happen everyday, but she had glimpsed a fierce desire to learn in the girl's eyes and wanted to guide her well in her journey to pick the most suitable sport.

'Okay, come here and sit. I will tell you the story of how I got into hockey.'

***

A FUN SPORTS FACT FOR YOU

Your body is like a growing tree, and sports help it grow strong and healthy. The more you move and play, the stronger your bones and muscles become—just like a superhero in training!

WE ALL
NEED
INSPIRATION!
CHAPTER
FOUR

Priyanka was often teased by other children because of her height. She was the tallest kid in her class, even taller than the tallest boy. This made her the butt of jokes for everyone. She tried to ignore the cruel jokes but some of the boys were very mean to her. The teachers were mostly apathetic to her plight. They didn't care if her classmates made fun of her. Frustrated by their lack of action, and angry at everyone else, Priyanka decided that she needed to silence them all.

But how? She didn't have many options other than fighting them, one at a time. That'd only get her into trouble and there was no certainty that she'd win over all the boys in her class. No, she needed to do something else; something significant that transformed her from a joke to an inspiration for all.

So, she started to look at her options. At first, Priyanka contemplated becoming a model. She'd certainly gain a lot of respect if she became a beauty queen and an object of fascination for the public. But that wasn't possible until she reached adulthood.

Priyanka knew that she didn't want to be a bookworm. Excelling at academics was nice, but even intelligent children were not immune to bullying, as she had seen in her own class. She turned her attention towards the only field that looked appropriate for a tall girl like her—sports!

She had to pick a sport, excel at it and show everyone what she was truly capable of.

However, she found a big obstacle even there. Her school's sports teacher, Mr Negi, was an ill-mannered man who abused children, physically and verbally, for fun. Priyanka did not want to engage with him in any way, whatsoever. She also knew that he wouldn't be able to help her either. Going by the dismal state of the school's cricket and football teams, she had no hopes of learning anything from that loser.

Her wish to find a suitable coach was fulfilled rather quickly and in a very unexpected way.

Gautam Singh, a hockey coach, was one of her neighbours. He taught at the Marx Sports Academy, and was always looking for more children to join the teams.

Curiously, Priyanka didn't have hockey in mind when she was hunting for a sport to play. Hockey, even while being the National sport, wasn't very popular and it was very difficult to find a good coach who'd teach it to you properly because it didn't pay well.

Priyanka had reached the limit of her patience and was starting to panic, when her brother, Himesh, reminded her of Gautam uncle.

'But hockey is boring, nobody even plays it!' Priyanka had complained to him.

'What's that?' remarked Himesh, raising his eyebrows. 'You just don't want to work hard.'

'That's not true at all!' Priyanka said, 'I don't have any interest in hockey.'

'Try it once,' Himesh suggested. 'If you dislike it, you can always quit.'

So, Priyanka had gone to the academy and signed up for a trial class.

Gautam sir, who was very glad to see Priyanka, told the girls to take twenty laps around the academy ground. And instantly, she realised how unfit she was. She hadn't even completed a full circle when she became breathless and her limbs felt like they were made of soggy wood and she started sweating through her clothes. Pushing herself to complete the laps felt foolish, because she knew that she'd faint if she kept going, but Priyanka knew that this was a chance to prove something, not only to Coach Gautam, but to herself as well. How could she even think of playing hockey if she couldn't even run twenty laps?

So Priyanka tried. She tried as hard as she could, and was able to complete 6 laps before her legs gave out and she fell on the ground.

Seeing her drop down, all the girls stopped immediately and helped her to her feet.

Coach Gautam rushed to her with a water bottle and told her to rest.

As she watched the girls train from the safety of the shed, Priyanka was overcome with a feeling that she hadn't encountered ever before. She really liked the focused energy and ferocity of the girls as they played. Each and every one of them had gone through what she *was going through but they had overcome their limitations and learnt something that they were passionate about.*

What she also discovered was that she wanted to do this not because she had something to prove to her classmates—that motive had already disappeared from her mind. She didn't have to prove to anyone, her worth as a human being. She'd stand up against her bullies and tell them to stop making fun of her. It had been foolish of her to give them so much power. She couldn't decide her life according to what other people made her feel.

She'd play hockey, and she'd play it well, because she wanted to do so. And that's what she did. Everyone was surprised when she returned for practice the next day and kept her promise of coming to practice daily. She'd be lying to herself if she said that it was all very easy. It wasn't easy at all, and there were times when she was very close to giving it up and going back to her life before hockey. It took her a while to start enjoying playing hockey, but when she did, it became easy for her to excel at it as well.

After spending months practising, Priyanka finally got a chance to show off her newly developed skills at a friendly match with another academy.

It was a Sunday, and to her surprise, some of her classmates who'd gotten word of the match had also come to watch her play. Priyanka was nervous, very nervous. In the changing room, her hands wouldn't stop shaking and she felt a heavy weight in her stomach that seemed to make her feel bloated and full.

'I don't feel good!' she moaned to her teammate, Supriya. 'I feel like vomiting!'

'Don't worry,' Supriya said, adding, 'You are going to be fine. Hockey is a team sport, so you won't have to do the heavy lifting on your own. Just pass the ball to any of us whenever it comes to you, if you are too scared to tackle the opponent.'

Priyanka nodded. She'd gone through the same drills as everyone on the team but she was aware of her inexperience. Nobody would blame her if she was unable to perform as well, but Priyanka wanted to do her best. The pressure to do her best was making her lose her wits. She went to the bathroom, tried to vomit but nothing came out of her mouth. Looking at her reflection in the mirror, Priyanka tried to focus and erase her fear.

She got back to the locker room, and then got dressed for the match and went to the field with her teammates. Priyanka stood at her spot at the back, and looked in the distance. She could see her parents sitting very near to the field in the stands and her classmates seated just a few rows above them.

The referee sounded the whistle and the field erupted into chaos as the girls started tackling each other for the ball. Priyanka knocked the edge of her hockey stick on the mushy ground and started pacing sideways, her eyes fixed on the ball.

It took only a few minutes for the ball to come rolling towards her, as one of her teammates, Tanu, passed it to her and shouted that she pass it to Meena, who was standing a few paces opposite her.

With an elegant sweep of her stick over the ball's side, Priyanka did as she was told, and passed the ball to Meena, who carried it to their opponent's part of the field. Meena passed it to Rachna, who secured a goal for their team with ease.

And with that, their team took the lead and went on to win the match!

Nobody could have been happier than Priyanka that day. She had finally achieved what she wanted. And it wasn't just that, as she realised that she loved playing hockey a lot. What had started as a mission to prove to her friends that she was worth more than their jokes had turned into a genuine interest and nothing could be better than that!

***

A FUN SPORTS FACT FOR YOU

Sports are like friendship factories! Every time you join a team or play with others, you're learning how to be a great teammate and make new friends. It's like having a second family who cheers you on!

SPORTS
IS
LIFE!
CHAPTER
FIVE

Neha was mesmerised by Priyanka's story. She felt inspired and energised, especially by her advice that one must not take up sports just to prove something to people. Neha didn't need to prove anything to anyone, but she had felt like a failure for not being able to choose a sport.

'I think I will take a trial class as well, Didi,' she told Priyanka.

She'd give hockey a try, and if that didn't work out, she'd try something else. What she'd learnt from Priyanka was an essential truth about sports and she felt very glad that she'd found it at the beginning of her journey.

Neha went back to her mother, and found her brother standing beside her.

'So, what did you choose?' Shanti asked her.

'I'll try hockey, Mummy,' she said, 'but if it doesn't work out, I'll go for another sport. I'll keep at it until I find my ideal sport.'

Shanti was surprised and glad by her daughter's reply. While Archit had been very quick in choosing karate, because he wanted to be stronger and more agile, her daughter had the better sense to try things until they fit her perfectly.

Overall, she was happy with both of their decisions and trusted that they'd be good at anything they tried.

As the evening turned into early night, and everyone started to file out of the academy, Archit and Neha stopped and looked back at the building.

Sports had never been an important part of their lives. They had treated it as an extra appendage that they could always remove from themselves and still live happily. Their mother's intervention had made them realise how wrong they were.

They were thankful for that, and also to the people whose stories they had heard at the academy, which had brought them to this moment of truth.

***

A FUN
SPORTS
FACT FOR
YOU

Sports are like puzzles that teach you to think fast and solve problems.

SPORTS
IS FOR
EVERYONE!
CHAPTER
SIX

Sankit sat cross-legged on the worn-out rug in his small living room, his eyes glued to the old television set. The screen flickered as Michael Phelps sliced through the water with the grace of a dolphin, his powerful strokes leaving a trail of ripples behind. Sankit's heart raced as he watched the legendary swimmer clinch yet another gold medal. The commentator's voice boomed, 'Phelps has done it again! A true champion of the water!' Sankit's eyes sparkled with admiration. He turned to his mother, Sunita, who was busy mending a tear in an old school uniform.

'Ma, I want to swim like him,' Sankit said, his voice trembling with excitement.

Sunita looked up, her hands pausing mid-stitch. She smiled softly, though her eyes betrayed a hint of worry. 'Swimming, beta? That's a big dream. But where will you learn? We don't have a pool nearby.'

Sankit's enthusiasm didn't waver. 'There are swimming classes in the big societies, Ma! I've seen the posters. They have huge pools and coaches who teach kids how to swim.'

Sunita's smile faded. She knew those posh, gated societies well. They were worlds apart from their modest two-room apartment in the bustling neighbourhood of Rajnagar. The fees for those swimming classes alone, were beyond their means. Her husband, Rajesh, worked long hours as a mechanic, while she took on odd tailoring jobs to make ends meet. Swimming lessons were a luxury they couldn't afford.

But Sankit had a determined look on his face and Sunita couldn't bear to crush his dreams. 'Let me see what we can do,' she said, her voice gentle, but firm.

The next day, Sunita set out on her old bicycle, determined to find a way for Sankit to learn swimming. She visited the posh societies, hoping to negotiate a lower fee or a scholarship. But the receptionists at the clubs were polite yet firm. 'Our fees are fixed, madam. We don't offer discounts,' one of them said, her tone dismissive.

Disheartened, Sunita returned home. That evening, as she prepared dinner, she overheard a neighbour talking about the Bhagat Singh Sports

Centre. 'They offer sports training for children from less-privileged backgrounds. And the fees are minimal.'

Sunita's heart leapt with hope. The next morning, she and Sankit made their way to the sports centre. The building was modest, its gate rusty, with paint peeling off its walls. But the energy inside was palpable. Children in worn-out sports gear practised badminton, ran on the track, and played football on a large field. At the far end of the complex was a giant, 50-metre swimming pool, its cool and inviting waters sparkling under the sun.

Sankit's eyes widened. 'Ma, look! A pool!' he said.

Sunita approached the reception desk, where a kind-looking man in his fifties sat. 'We'd like to enrol my son in swimming classes,' she said, her voice tinged with hope.

The man smiled warmly. 'Of course. We're here to help all children. The fees are nominal, and we provide all the necessary equipment.'

Sankit's face lit up. He could hardly believe his luck. That very day, he was introduced to Coach

Ramesh, a former national-level swimmer who had dedicated his life to training underprivileged children.

The first day at the pool was both thrilling and terrifying for Sankit. The water felt colder than he had imagined and his legs wobbled as he stood at the edge. Coach Ramesh noticed his hesitation and knelt beside him. 'Fear is natural, Sankit. But remember, every champion was once a beginner. Take it one step at a time.'

With those words of encouragement, Sankit took his first plunge. The water enveloped him, and though he flailed and gasped, he felt a strange sense of exhilaration. Over the weeks, he learned to float, kick, and eventually swim. Coach Ramesh was a patient teacher, pushing Sankit to improve his strokes while celebrating every small victory.

Sankit's progress was remarkable. He practised tirelessly, often staying late after class to perfect his strokes. His parents, though exhausted from their daily struggles, made sure to support him. Sunita would pack his lunch early in the morning, and

Rajesh would drop him off at the sports centre before heading to work.

One day, as Sankit was practising his backstroke, a group of children from one of the posh societies arrived at the pool. They were there for a friendly competition organised by their coach. Sankit watched as they jumped into the water with confidence, their sleek swimsuits and goggles a stark contrast to his modest attire.

One of the boys, Arjun, noticed Sankit and smirked. 'Hey, kid, you think you can swim with us? This isn't a kiddie pool, you know.'

Sankit clenched his fists but remained silent. Coach Ramesh placed a reassuring hand on his shoulder. 'Don't let their words get to you, Sankit. The water doesn't care where you come from. It only cares how well you swim.'

The competition began, and Sankit found himself pitted against Arjun and the others in a 50-metre freestyle race. As the whistle blew, Sankit dived into the water with all the strength he could muster. His strokes were powerful and precise, his focus unwavering. The other children were fast, but Sankit's determination gave him an edge.

The crowd cheered as Sankit touched the wall a split second before Arjun. He had won! Arjun stared at him in disbelief, while the other children clapped hesitantly. Coach Ramesh beamed with pride. 'Well done, Sankit! You've proven that talent knows no boundaries.'

Word of Sankit's victory spread quickly. The children from the posh societies, who had once looked down on him, now regarded him with respect. Arjun even approached him after the race. 'You're really good, Sankit. Maybe we can practice together sometime.'

Sankit smiled. 'Sure. The pool is for everyone.'

That evening, as Sankit returned home, his parents greeted him with tears of joy. Sunita hugged him tightly. 'We're so proud of you, Beta. You've shown us that dreams can come true, no matter how big they are.'

Sankit looked at his mother, his heart swelling with gratitude. 'It's because of you, Ma. You never gave up on me.'

From that day on, Sankit's life changed. He continued to train at the Bhagat Singh Sports Centre, his swimming skills improving with each passing day. He participated in more competitions, often winning medals and trophies. But more importantly, he became an inspiration to the other children in his neighbourhood, proving that with hard work and determination, even the biggest dreams are within reach.

Years later, when Sankit stood on the podium at a national swimming championship, he thought back to that day when he had first watched Michael Phelps on TV. He had come a long way from the boy who had dreamed of swimming in a posh society pool. And as the national anthem played, he knew that his journey was just beginning. The ripple of his dreams had become a wave, carrying him toward a future filled with endless possibilities.

***

TEAMWORK
IS THE KEY
TO SUCCESS!
CHAPTER
SEVEN

Namita adjusted her tennis visor and gripped her racket tightly as she watched Sneha practise her serves on the adjacent court. The rhythmic thud of the ball hitting the racket echoed across the school tennis courts, but Namita's focus was elsewhere. She couldn't help but feel a pang of irritation every time Sneha's confident laughter reached her ears. Sneha was everything Namita wasn't—outgoing, effortlessly popular, and, worst of all, good at tennis, too.

The two had been rivals since they had turned seven years of age, when Namita had narrowly beaten Sneha in the school singles championship. Since then, their rivalry had only intensified. Namita was convinced that Sneha was out to sabotage her, whether it was by hogging the best practice slots or while making snide remarks about her technique.

So, when their coach, Ms Kapoor, announced that they would be representing the school together in the upcoming doubles competition, Namita was visibly ruffled.

'Doubles? With her?' Namita had blurted out, unable to hide her dismay.

Ms Kapoor had raised an eyebrow. 'Yes, Namita. Doubles requires teamwork, and I believe the two of you have the potential to be a formidable pair. If you can put your differences aside, that is.'

Namita had reluctantly agreed, but the first few practice sessions had been a disaster. They couldn't coordinate their moves, and their communication on the court was non-existent. Namita was convinced that Sneha was deliberately playing poorly to make her look bad.

'You're supposed to cover the net, not stand there like a statue!' Namita snapped during one particularly frustrating session.

Sneha rolled her eyes. 'Maybe if you didn't hog all the shots, I'd actually have something to do!'

Their bickering became so frequent that Mrs Kapoor had to intervene. 'Girls, this isn't just about you. You're representing the school. If you can't work together, we'll have to find another pair.'

The threat of being replaced was enough to make them both quiet down, but the tension between them remained palpable.

One crisp autumn afternoon, during a particularly intense practice session, disaster struck. Namita was sprinting to return a powerful shot from Sneha when her foot caught on a loose patch of turf. She stumbled and fell, landing awkwardly on her ankle.

A sharp pain shot through her leg, and she let out a cry.

Sneha immediately dropped her racket and rushed over. 'Namita! Are you okay?'

Namita winced as she tried to stand. 'I'm fine,' she muttered, though the pain in her ankle suggested otherwise.

Ms Kapoor hurried over, her face etched with concern. 'That doesn't look fine. Sneha, take her to the nurse's office. Now.'

Sneha didn't hesitate. She slung Namita's arm over her shoulder and helped her limp off the court. Namita wanted to protest, to insist that she could manage on her own, but the pain was too intense. Reluctantly, she leaned on Sneha as they made their way to the school nurse.

The nurse examined Namita's ankle and recommended a visit to the doctor for an X-ray. 'It might just be a sprain, but it's best to get it checked,' she said.

Sneha offered to accompany Namita to the clinic. 'My mum can drive us. She's picking me up in a few minutes anyway.'

Namita was about to refuse, but the thought of navigating the journey alone was daunting. 'Fine,' she said curtly.

The car ride to the clinic was awkward at first. Namita sat in silence, staring out the window, while Sneha made small talk with her mother. But as the minutes passed, Namita couldn't help but notice how kind Sneha was being. She even offered to carry Namita's bag when they arrived at the clinic.

'You don't have to do that,' Namita said, though her tone was less sharp than usual.

Sneha shrugged. 'It's no big deal. You're injured, and I'm just trying to help.'

At the clinic, Sneha stayed by Namita's side, filling out forms and keeping her company while they waited for the doctor. When the X-ray confirmed that it was just a sprain, Namita felt a wave of relief.

'You'll need to rest it for a few days,' the doctor advised. 'No tennis until it heals.'

Namita's heart sank. The doubles competition was only two weeks away. How would they practice if she couldn't even hold a racket?

Sneha seemed to read her thoughts. 'Don't worry,' she said as they left the clinic.

'We'll figure it out. Maybe we can work on strategy and coordination off the court until you're better.'

Namita looked at Sneha, surprised by her supportive tone. 'Why are you being so nice to me?' she blurted out.

Sneha laughed. 'Because we're a team, aren't we? And teammates look out for each other.'

Namita felt a pang of guilt. She had been so quick to assume the worst about Sneha, but maybe she had been wrong. 'I'm sorry,' she said quietly. 'I thought you were trying to sabotage me.'

Sneha's eyes widened. 'What? Why would I do that? I mean, sure, we're rivals, but that doesn't mean I want you to fail. If anything, I want to beat you, fair and square.'

Namita smiled for the first time that day. 'Fair enough.'

Over the next few days, Namita and Sneha began to bond. They spent hours discussing strategies, analysing their opponents' strengths and weaknesses, and even watching videos of professional doubles matches together. Namita was surprised to discover that Sneha was just as passionate about tennis as she was, and that they shared a lot in common beyond the court.

When Namita's ankle healed enough for her to return to practice, their teamwork had improved dramatically. They moved in sync, anticipating each other's moves and communicated seamlessly. Mrs Kapoor was impressed. 'Now that's what I call teamwork,' she said with a smile.

The day of the doubles competition arrived, and the atmosphere was electric. Namita and Sneha walked onto the court together, their confidence radiating. Their opponents were a formidable pair from a rival school, but Namita and Sneha were ready.

The match was intense, with both teams trading powerful shots and clever strategies. But Namita and Sneha's newfound synergy gave them the edge. They covered the court effortlessly, supporting each other at every turn. When the final point was won, the crowd erupted in applause.

Namita and Sneha hugged, their faces beaming with joy. 'We did it!' Namita exclaimed.

'Of course we did,' Sneha replied with a grin. 'We're unstoppable when we work together.'

As they stood on the podium, holding their trophy, Namita felt a surge of gratitude. She had not only won a championship but also gained a friend. The rivalry that had once defined their relationship now seemed trivial compared to the bond they had forged.

On the way home, Namita turned to Sneha. 'Thanks for being such a great partner.'

Sneha smiled. 'Anytime. But don't think this means I'm going easy on you in the singles matches.'

Namita laughed. 'Wouldn't dream of it.'

Together, they had proven that even the fiercest rivals could become the strongest teammates.

***

BELIEVE IN
YOURSELF!

CHAPTER
EIGHT

Udit sat on the edge of the school football field, his knees pulled up to his chest, watching his teammates practice. The sound of cleats crunching against the grass and the occasional shout of 'Pass!' or 'Shoot!' filled the air, but Udit felt disconnected from it all. He used to love football—the thrill of dribbling past defenders, the satisfaction of scoring a goal, the camaraderie of being part of a team. But lately, it had all felt like a chore. He was just an average player, and no matter how hard he tried, he couldn't seem to improve. The spark that once drove him had fizzled out, leaving him feeling empty and unmotivated.

'Udit, come on! We need you for the drill!' called out Rohan, the team captain.

Udit forced a smile and jogged over, but his heart wasn't in it. He went through the motions, passing the ball half-heartedly and missing an easy shot on the goal. Rohan gave him a puzzled look but didn't say anything. Udit knew he was letting the team down, but he couldn't help it. He just didn't understand why he had lost his energy and inspiration.

That evening, as Udit walked back to his housing society, he heard the familiar thud of a football being kicked. He followed the sound and saw a group of kids playing in the small park near the entrance. They couldn't have been more than eight or nine years old, and their game was chaotic at best. The ball bounced awkwardly, passes went astray, and there was more running in circles than actual play. But what struck Udit was the sheer joy on their faces. They were laughing, shouting, and having the time of their lives.

Udit stood there for a while, watching them. Then, on an impulse, he walked over. 'Hey, can I join?' he asked.

The kids stopped and looked at him, wide-eyed. One of them, a boy with a mop of curly hair, grinned. 'Sure! But we're not very good.'

'That's okay,' Udit said, smiling. 'Maybe I can help you get better.'

The kids exchanged excited glances. 'Really? You'll teach us?' asked another boy, his eyes shining with hope.

Udit nodded. 'Why not? Let's start with the basics.'

From that day on, Udit began training the kids every evening after school. He started with simple drills—passing, dribbling, and shooting. The kids were eager to learn, and their enthusiasm was infectious. Udit found himself looking forward to their sessions, something he hadn't felt in a long time.

One evening, as they were practising, one of the kids, a girl named Priya, asked, 'Udit Bhaiya, why don't you play for a big team? You're so good!'

Udit chuckled. 'I'm not that good, Priya. I'm just an average player.'

'But you're amazing to us!' said the curly-haired boy, Arjun. 'You know so much about football. You should play more!'

Udit didn't know how to respond. He had always thought of himself as mediocre, but to these kids, he was a star. Their admiration made him see himself in a new light.

A few weeks later, Udit heard about an inter-society football competition. It was a small event, but it seemed like the perfect opportunity for the kids to showcase what they had learned. He brought it up during their practice.

'How would you all like to play in a real match?' he asked.

The kids erupted in excitement. 'A real match? With uniforms and everything?' Arjun asked, his eyes wide.

'Yes, with uniforms and everything,' Udit said, laughing. 'But we'll have to work really hard to prepare. Are you up for it?'

'Yes!' they shouted in unison.

Udit threw himself into training them with renewed vigour. He taught them formations, strategies, and how to work as a team. The kids improved rapidly, and Udit felt a sense of pride he hadn't experienced in years. He realised that teaching them had reignited his own love for football. The spark was back.

The day of the competition arrived, and Udit's team—dubbed the 'Park Panthers'—was ready. They were up against teams from other societies, many of whom were older and more experienced. But Udit had drilled his team well, and they played with heart.

The first match was tough, but the Panthers managed to win 2-1, thanks to a last-minute goal by Priya. The kids celebrated wildly, and Udit felt a lump in his throat. They had done it.

The second match was even harder, but the Panthers held their ground. Arjun scored a stunning goal, and their defence, led by a boy named Ravi, was impenetrable. They won, 1-0.

By the time they reached the final, the Panthers were exhausted but determined. Their opponents were a strong team from the neighbouring society, but Udit's team played the match of their lives. The score was tied 1-1 until the final minute, when Arjun dribbled past two defenders and scored the winning goal.

The crowd erupted in cheers, and the kids rushed to Udit, hugging him and jumping up and down. 'We won, Udit Bhaiya! We won!' they shouted.

Udit's eyes filled with tears. 'You were brilliant,' he said. 'I'm so proud of you all.'

That night, as Udit lay in bed, he thought about everything. Teaching the kids had not only brought back his love for football but also shown him that he was capable of more than he had ever believed. He realised that he had been holding himself back, afraid of failure. But now, he felt ready to push himself and become the player he had always wanted to be.

The next day, Udit approached his school coach. 'Sir, I want to improve. I want to be the best player I can be. Will you help me?'

The coach smiled. 'I was wondering when you'd ask. Of course, Udit. Let's get to work.'

From that day on, Udit trained harder than ever. He practised before school, stayed late after practice, and even worked on his fitness at home. His teammates noticed the change and rallied around him, offering support and encouragement.

Months later, Udit's hard work paid off. He scored the winning goal in the inter-school championship, securing victory for his team. As he stood on the field, surrounded by cheering teammates, he knew that he had finally found his spark again.

And it all started with a group of kids who believed in him, even when he didn't believe in himself.

***

NEVER GIVE UP ON YOUR DREAMS!

CHAPTER NINE

Himesh stood in front of the mirror, holding his cricket bat like it was a sword. He swung it gently, imagining himself hitting the winning six in a packed stadium, the crowd roaring his name. In his mind, he was Mahendra Singh Dhoni, calm under pressure, leading his team to victory. Cricket wasn't just a game for Himesh—it was his dream, his passion, his escape. But lately, that dream felt like it was slipping away.

'Himesh! Have you finished your maths assignment?' his mother called from the living room.

Himesh sighed and put the bat down. 'Almost, Ma,' he replied, though he hadn't even started. He glanced at the pile of textbooks on his desk and felt a knot tighten in his stomach. His parents had made it clear—cricket was a hobby, not a career. Their dream for him was a corporate law degree, a stable job, and a life of financial security. But every time Himesh thought about sitting in an office, wearing a suit and tie, he felt like he was suffocating.

'You can't make a living playing cricket,' his father had said during their last argument. 'Focus on your studies. That's what will take you places.'

Himesh had tried to explain how much cricket meant to him, but his words fell on deaf ears. 'You'll thank us later,' his mother had added, her tone final.

But Himesh wasn't ready to give up. He had a plan. The district cricket trials were just a week away, and he was determined to prove himself. If he could get selected, maybe his parents would see that cricket wasn't just a childish dream—it was his future.

The only problem was time. Between school, tuition, and his parents' constant reminders to study, Himesh barely had a moment to practice. He started waking up at 5 am to sneak in an hour of batting practice before school. He'd rush to the local park with his bat and a few balls, using the boundary wall as a makeshift net. His best friend, Jatin, used to join him, but lately, Himesh had been too focused to even talk to him.

'Hey, Himesh! Wait up!' Jatin called one morning as Himesh hurried out of the house.

'Not today, Jatin,' Himesh said without stopping. 'I've got to practice.'

Jatin frowned. 'You've been saying that for weeks. When are we going to hang out like we used to?'

Himesh hesitated. He missed their long conversations and silly jokes, but he couldn't afford distractions. 'After the trials,' he promised. 'I just need to focus right now.'

Jatin looked hurt but nodded. 'Alright. Good luck, I guess.'

The day of the trials arrived, and Himesh felt a mix of excitement and nerves. The ground was buzzing with young cricketers, all vying for a spot on the district team. Himesh took a deep breath and reminded himself why he was there. This was his chance to prove himself—not just to his parents, but to himself.

The trials began with a batting session. Himesh stepped up to the crease, his grip firm on the bat. The first ball came speeding towards him, and he swung with precision, sending it soaring over the boundary. The next few balls were equally well-timed, and soon, the selectors were nodding appreciatively.

Next was the fielding test. Himesh dived to stop a powerful shot, his reflexes sharp and his movements agile. He could hear murmurs of approval from the sidelines. Finally, it was time for the bowling session. Though batting was his strength, Himesh had been practising his spin bowling relentlessly. He delivered a series of tricky spins that left the batsmen struggling.

By the end of the trials, Himesh was exhausted but exhilarated. He had given it his all, and it showed. The head selector called him over. 'You've got talent, son. We'd like to offer you a spot on the district team.'

Himesh's heart leapt. 'Thank you, sir!' he said, barely able to contain his excitement.

That evening, Himesh walked into the house, clutching the selection letter like it was a trophy. His parents were in the living room, discussing his upcoming tuition schedule. He took a deep breath and stepped forward.

'Ma, Papa, I need to talk to you,' he said, his voice steady.

His father looked up, frowning. 'What is it, Himesh? Have you finished your homework?'

Himesh handed him the letter. 'I got selected for the district cricket team.'

There was a moment of stunned silence. His mother was the first to speak. 'Cricket team? When did you even have time for trials?'

'I've been practising every morning,' Himesh admitted. 'I know you want me to focus on studies, but cricket is my passion. I'm good at it, and I want to pursue it as a career.'

His father's expression softened as he read the letter. 'This is... impressive, Himesh. But what about your future? Cricket is unpredictable.'

'I know it's a risk,' Himesh said, 'but it's a risk I'm willing to take. Please, just give me a chance to follow my dream.'

His parents exchanged a look. Finally, his father sighed. 'If this is what you truly want, we'll support you. But you have to promise to balance it with your studies.'

Himesh's eyes lit up. 'I promise! Thank you, Papa, Ma!'

With his parents' blessing, Himesh felt like a weight had been lifted off his shoulders. But there was one more thing he needed to do. He grabbed his phone and called Jatin.

'Hey, Jatin. Can we talk?'

There was a pause. 'Sure. What's up?'

'I'm sorry,' Himesh said. 'I've been so focused on cricket that I ignored you. You're my best friend, and I shouldn't have pushed you away.'

Jatin chuckled. 'It's okay, Himesh. I get it. You were chasing your dream. So, how did the trials go?'

'I got selected!' Himesh said, grinning.

'That's amazing! Let's celebrate. My treat.'

That weekend, Himesh and Jatin threw a small party with their friends. They played cricket in the park, laughed over old memories, and celebrated Himesh's selection. As the sun set, Himesh felt a deep sense of gratitude. He had his parents' support, his best friend back, and a chance to chase his dream.

'To Himesh, the future Dhoni!' Jatin said, raising a glass of lemonade.

'To dreams and friendship!' Himesh added, clinking his glass against Jatin's.

As they laughed and cheered, Himesh knew that this was just the beginning. With hard work, determination, and the support of his loved ones, he was ready to take on the world—one match at a time.

***

Trivia and
Fun
Activities
for You!

FAMOUS INDIAN SPORTS PERSONALITIES

Milkha Singh (Athletics): *Known as the 'Flying Sikh,' he was a legendary runner who overcame incredible challenges. His life story is so inspiring that a whole movie was made about him, titled 'Bhaag Milkha Bhaag.'*

Sachin Tendulkar (Cricket): *Known as the 'Little Master,' Sachin is like a superhero of cricket! He's the most famous cricket player in India, who played for 24 years and scored more runs than almost anyone else in the world. Kids love him because he started playing cricket when he was super young and became a legend.*

Mary Kom (Boxing): *A boxing champion who is also a mom! She's from the northeastern state of Manipur and has won multiple world championships. Her story shows kids that with hard work and dedication, you can achieve anything.*

Sania Mirza (Tennis): *A tennis star who became world number one in doubles. She broke many barriers and showed that Indian women can excel in any sport they choose.*

Abhinav Bindra (Shooting): *India's first individual Olympic gold medallist in shooting. He proves that sports isn't just about physical strength, but also about focus, precision, and mental toughness.*

MS Dhoni (Cricket): Captain Cool, as everyone calls him, is a cricket wizard who led India to win the World Cup in 2011. He's famous for his calm attitude and amazing skills behind the wickets. Kids admire him because he makes difficult things look easy and always stays cool under pressure.

Bajrang Punia (Wrestling): A young wrestling champion who has won medals in international competitions. He shows kids that wrestling is an exciting sport where Indian athletes can shine globally.

Virat Kohli (Cricket): The current king of cricket, Virat is known for his incredible energy and passion. He's super fit, scores tons of runs, and is a role model for young cricketers who want to be strong and determined.

PV Sindhu (Badminton): A girl who showed the world that women can be incredible sports champions! She won a silver medal at the Olympics and has made India proud in badminton. She's an inspiration for young girls who dream of becoming athletes.

Neeraj Chopra (Javelin Throw): A young athlete who won India's first Olympic gold medal in athletics. His victory made the entire country proud and inspired many young sports enthusiasts to try track and field events.

Sunil Chhetri (Football): India's greatest football player and the captain of the Indian national team. Known for his incredible speed, powerful kicks, and leadership on the field, Sunil has scored more goals for India than any other player in history.

MOVIES THAT WILL INSPIRE YOU!

Chak De! India (2007)

Meet Coach Kabir and his amazing team of hockey players! Watch as girls from different parts of India come together, learn to play as one team, and chase their dreams of winning for their country. Full of excitement, friendship, and heart-pumping hockey action!

Iqbal (2005)

Meet Iqbal, a boy who dreams of bowling fast cricket balls! Though he can't hear or speak, his love for cricket speaks louder than words. With help from a special coach and his loving sister, Iqbal shows that big dreams come true when you never stop trying.

Dangal (2016)

Sisters Geeta and Babita discover they're natural-born wrestlers! With their papa as their coach, they tumble their way from their small village to becoming champions. It's a true story!

Mary Kom (2014)

The amazing story of a super-strong girl who punches her way to glory! Mary starts as a small-town girl who loves boxing and becomes one of the world's best boxers. She shows that with a big heart and brave spirit, you can knock down any obstacle in life!

Lagaan (2001)

A village full of farmers learn to play cricket to save their home! Watch them learn this new game from scratch—how to bat, bowl, and catch. With music, dancing, and edge-of-your-seat cricket matches, this story shows how sports can bring everyone together!

Space Jam (1996)

Basketball superstar Michael Jordan teams up with Bugs Bunny and the Looney Tunes gang for the most incredible game ever! With silly jokes, awesome basketball moves, and cartoon fun, this adventure shows that the best teams can come in surprising packages!

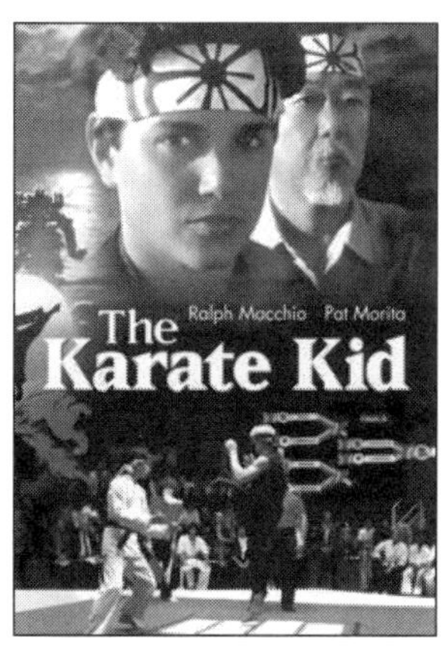

The Karate Kid (1984)

Daniel moves to a new town and learns karate from Mr Miyagi, the wisest and coolest teacher ever! Through fun training like "wax on, wax off," Daniel learns that karate is about more than just kicking and punching—it's about believing in yourself!

McFarland USA (2015)

In a small town where everyone works hard picking fruits and vegetables, the kids use their speed and determination to become champions. It's a true story about running toward your dreams!

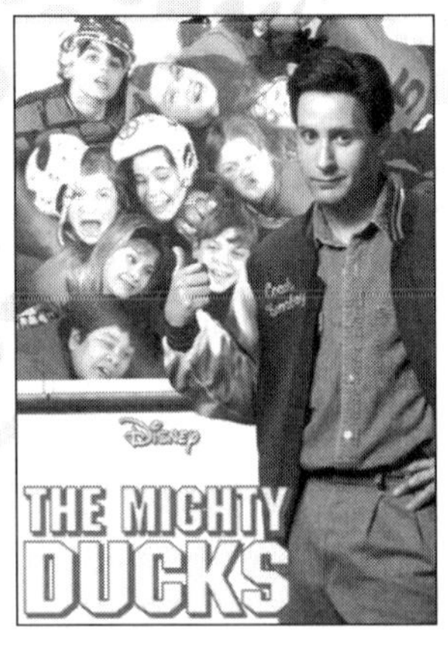

The Mighty Ducks (1992)

A bunch of kids who aren't very good at hockey meet a coach who changes everything! Together, they learn to skate, score, and most importantly, work as a team. With lots of fun, funny moments, and exciting games, they become the mightiest team around!

Hawaa Hawaai (2014)

This is a heartwarming story about Arjun, a young boy who falls in love with skating after watching kids practice at a skating rink. Though he can't afford fancy skates, he doesn't give up! With help from his loyal friends who build him makeshift roller skates from scraps, and a kind coach who believes in him, Arjun rolls his way toward becoming a champion skater. The movie is full of friendship and creativity, and shows how dreams can come true even when you start with nothing but determination!

INSPIRING
YOUR CHILD
TO
EMBRACE
SPORTS

- **Make it fun:** *Sports should feel like play, not a chore. Choose activities that look enjoyable and exciting to your child. Don't push too hard or make it feel like work.*

- **Lead by example:** *Kids often want to do what their parents do. Show enthusiasm for physical activity. Exercise together, play games outside, or share your own sports experiences.*

- **Try different sports:** *Children have unique interests. Let them explore various sports like soccer, basketball, swimming, martial arts, or dance. Don't force them into one specific activity.*

- **Focus on enjoyment, not performance:** *Praise effort and fun. Celebrate their participation, teamwork, and personal improvement. This helps build confidence and positive feelings about sports.*

- **Start young and keep it light:** *Introduce sports early as playful activities. Use simple games and basic skills that feel more like playing than serious training.*

- **Watch sports together:** Share exciting matches or games on TV. Talk about interesting moments, athletes, and what makes the sport exciting. This can spark their curiosity.

- **Listen to their preferences:** Ask what sports they might want to try. Pay attention to their natural interests and energy levels.

- **Remove pressure:** Never criticise or make them feel bad about their performance. Sports should be about joy, health, and personal growth.

- **Provide support:** Offer to help them practice, buy proper equipment, or sign them up for classes if they're interested.

- **Understand individual differences:** Some kids are naturally athletic, while others might prefer less competitive activities. Respect their unique personality and comfort level.

SOMETIMES YOU WIN, ALWAYS YOU LEARN!

Being a Good Sport

Winning feels amazing—like getting a birthday present! But losing can feel like a rainy day. The cool part? You can shine no matter what! When you win, give high-fives and say, 'Good game!' to the other team. When you lose, smile and say, 'Congratulations!' Remember, being kind and respectful is more important than any trophy.

Losing: Your Secret Teacher

Think of losing like getting a puzzle wrong the first time—it helps you figure out which pieces need to be moved! Every time things don't go your way, you gain new skills. Maybe you discover a better way to throw a ball or realise you need to run faster. These little lessons are like secret tips that help you improve at your sport!

Practice Makes Progress

Remember learning to ride a bike? You probably fell a few times before you got it right! Sports work the same way. The more you practice, the better you get.

It's like building with blocks—sometimes they fall, but every time you rebuild, you get stronger. Keep trying, and one day you'll surprise yourself with how much you've learned!

Bounce-Back Power

Think of yourself as a bouncy ball—when you fall, you bounce right back up! This is called resilience. Every time you keep playing after a tough game or try again after missing a shot, your bounce-back power gets stronger. It's like having a secret superpower that helps you never give up, no matter what happens.

The Biggest Win? Having Fun

The most important thing isn't whether you win or lose—it's about how much fun you have and how much you learn along the way! Even the best athletes in the world lose sometimes, but they keep smiling, learning, and giving their best effort.

Being the Boss of Your Time

Just like you wouldn't eat all your Diwali sweets at once, you need to plan your time wisely! Sports teach you to be a time ninja—knowing when to practice, when to do homework, and when to rest. It's like having a special calendar in your head that helps you balance fun and important tasks every day.

Setting Goals: Your Treasure Map to Success

Want to score more goals? Run faster? Jump higher? That's goal setting! Start with small steps—like practising for 15 minutes a day. Think of it like climbing a ladder, taking one step at a time. Each small achievement gets you closer to your big dream, just like following a treasure map to find something amazing!

Rules: The Traffic Lights of Sports

Rules in sports are just like traffic lights—they keep everyone safe and help the game run smoothly. Learning to follow rules on the field also helps you follow them at home and school. It's like being a superhero who knows exactly when to stop, go, and await their turn!

Growing Your Confidence Power

Every time you try something new in sports, your confidence grows stronger! It's like a special muscle that gets bigger each time you use it. Whether you're learning a new move, missing a shot but trying again, or encouraging your teammates, you're building confidence. Soon, you'll feel brave enough to tackle any challenge!

Being a Leader: The Team Captain Mindset

Leaders are like team captains—they help others do their best! You can be a leader by cheering on your teammates, sharing what you know, and showing good sportsmanship. It's like being the star of a movie who helps everyone else shine too!

Superpower Skills for Life

The skills you learn in sports are like superpowers that help you in school, at home, and everywhere else in life. The more you practice them, the stronger they get! Keep playing, learning, and growing—you're becoming unstoppable!

Playing Together is Super Fun

Think of a team like your favourite sandwich—every ingredient makes it better! When you play with others, you can do amazing things that wouldn't be possible alone. It's like building with LEGO blocks—a block by itself may be nice, but when you put them all together, you can create something incredible! Playing with teammates means more laughs, more high-fives, and more fun for everyone.

Sharing and Working Together

Being on a team is like being in a band—everyone has an important part to play! Sometimes you'll pass the ball, sometimes you'll catch it. Sometimes you'll be the helper, and sometimes you'll be the one scoring. Sharing the spotlight and working together makes the whole team stronger. It's like making music—when everyone plays their instrument just right, it sounds amazing!

Everyone Has a Special Role

On a team, everyone has their own superpower! Some people are great at running fast, others at throwing far, and some at coming up with clever strategies. It's like being part of a superhero team—each hero has different powers, but together they save the day! Understanding your role means knowing when to use your superpower and when to let your teammates use theirs.

Being a Great Teammate

Supporting your teammates is like being a cheerleader and a player at the same time! When someone feels down, you can give them a high-five and say, 'You've got this!' When a teammate does something great, celebrate with them. If someone makes a mistake, help them shake it off. It's like having a team of friends who always have your back—and you have theirs too!

Making Magic Together

Just like bees work together to make honey, teams work together to create something special. Every

person on the team matters, and together, you can do incredible things!

Making Your Body Happy

Did you know your body loves to move? It's true! When you run, jump, or dance, your body sends you happy signals—like tiny fireworks of joy inside! Sometimes you might feel butterflies in your tummy when you're excited, or your heart might beat faster when you're having fun. That's your body's way of saying, 'Yay! We're moving!'

Fun is the Best Prize

Winning games is nice, but having fun is even better! Think about playing with bubbles—it doesn't matter if you pop them all, what matters is how much you laugh while trying. Sports are just the same! When you focus on having fun, every game becomes an adventure. Whether you score a goal or not, if you're smiling, you're winning!

So Many Ways to Move and Groove

There are tons of fun ways to be active! You can:

- Dance like nobody's watching
- Play catch with friends
- Have a silly race with your family
- Make up your own games
- Jump rope while singing
- Play hopscotch
- Have a hula hoop contest
  It's like having a giant toy box full of different ways to move—try them all and find your favourites!

Making Happy Memories

Every time you play sports, you're collecting special memories—like seashells on a beach! Maybe it's the time you and your friends couldn't stop laughing during a game, or when your whole family played soccer in the backyard. These happy memories are treasures you can keep forever. Years from now, you'll remember these fun times and smile!

Feel Your Best

Moving your body isn't about being the best—it's about feeling your best! When you're having fun while being active, you're doing it exactly right!

HOW WELL DO YOU KNOW INDIAN SPORTS?

Test your knowledge with this fun quiz!

1. How many Olympic gold medals has India won in field hockey?

   A)   5
   B)   8
   C)   10
   D)   12

2. Which Indian cricketer holds the record for the highest individual score in a One Day International (ODI) match?

   A)   Virat Kohli
   B)   M S Dhoni
   C)   Rohit Sharma
   D)   Sachin Tendulkar

3. Who was India's first Grandmaster in chess?

   A)   Koneru Humpy
   B)   Rameshbabu Praggnanandhaa
   C)   Vishwanathan Anand
   D)   Pentala Harikrishna

4. Which Indian athlete is known as the 'Payyoli Express'?

   A)   Hima Das
   B)   P T Usha
   C)   Dutee Chand
   D)   Anju Bobby George

5. How many times has India won the Kabaddi World Cup in the men's category?

    A)   3
    B)   5
    C)   7
    D)   It has won everytime

6. In which year did India reach the semi-finals of the Olympics in football?

    A)   1956
    B)   1964
    C)   1982
    D)   1996

7. Kushti (Indian wrestling) has been practised in India for how many years?

    A)   1,000 years
    B)   2,500 years
    C)   500 years
    D)   3,000 years

8. Mirabai Chanu won a silver medal at the Tokyo Olympics in which sport?

    A)   Wrestling
    B)   Weightlifting
    C)   Boxing
    D)   Shooting

9. Who was the first Indian to win an individual Olympic medal?

    A)   K D Jadhav
    B)   Abhinav Bindra
    C)   P V Sindhu
    D)   Sushil Kumar

10. Who was the first Indian woman to climb Mount Everest?

    A)   Arunima Sinha
    B)   Santosh Yadav
    C)   Bachendri Pal
    D)   Lhotse Sherpa

11. In which year did India win its first Cricket World Cup?

    A)   1979
    B)   1983
    C)   1996
    D)   2011

12. Kapil Dev once scored a Test century in how many balls, setting a record at that time?

    A)   50
    B)   55
    C)   74
    D)   60

13. Who was India's first Formula 1 driver?

    A) Jehan Daruvala
    B) Karun Chandhok
    C) Narain Karthikeyan
    D) Armaan Ebrahim

14. Which Indian athlete has won two Paralympic gold medals in javelin throw?

    A) Mariyappan Thangavelu
    B) Devendra Jhajharia
    C) Avani Lekhara
    D) Deepa Malik

15. At what age did Sachin Tendulkar make his debut for India?

    A) 14
    B) 16
    C) 18
    D) 20

Answers:

1. B ✓   2. C ✓   3. C ✓

4. B ✓   5. D ✓   6. A ✓

7. D ✓   8. B ✓   9. A ✓

10. C ✓   11. B ✓   12. C ✓

13. C ✓   14. B ✓   15. B ✓